OVER MY DEAD BODY

A GUIDE TO BIBLICAL MANHOOD

JUSTICE COLEMAN

Over My Dead Body
A Guide to Biblical Manhood
Justice Coleman
Copyright © 2019, by Justice Coleman

Printed in the United States of America
1 2 3 4 5 22 21 20 19

To my parents, Roy and Genny Coleman, for training me for manhood. To my in-laws, Rudy and Myra Oliva, for training me to be a pastor. When in doubt, I always look to your examples. I have always followed you, as you followed Christ.

TABLE OF CONTENTS

INTRODUCTION

There I was, frantically pacing around the men's bathroom of a small wedding chapel, tripping out like I was holding a grenade without a pin.

What am I thinking? Am I making the right decision? How would I know if I wasn't? Who gets married at 22 years old? Am I even a man yet?

I barely shave once a week.

How do I know I'm ready to make the biggest decision of my life?

Somebody get my mom.

Just then my mom came bursting through the doors. She looked beautiful in her salmon-colored dress and Texas-sized jewelry. She didn't care if it was the men's restroom; she was not looking for a man, she was looking for her boy.

"Mom! I'm so glad you are here. I need your help. The ceremony starts in 15 minutes and I'm freaking out. Just tell me I'm making the right decision." What my mother said next, without hesitation, did not exactly instill the confidence I was looking for.

"Son, it sounds like you're having second thoughts about getting married today. Here is what I am going to do. I am going to pull my car around back of this wedding chapel. You head out that side door and meet me there in five minutes. We will head straight to the airport and get you out of here. Don't worry about the cost of this wedding. I will cover the cost of the whole thing. I don't want you to make a decision today that you will regret the rest of your life."

I love my mom with all my heart. But, I had to look her right in the eyes and say, "Will you go get dad?"

My mom's advice was full of love; I'm sure you can hear that. She wanted to give me a way out. She wanted to save her boy from potentially making the biggest mistake of his life.

A few minutes later, my dad came into the restroom and my mom nervously left for the courtyard of family and friends.

"What is it, Son? Cold feet?"

"Dad, how do I know I'm making the right decision? I'm only 22 years old. Should I be getting married?"

My dad stayed silent. He leaned against the door of the bathroom stall in no hurry to give me an answer. He knew what he said next would have serious impact on my life.

"Have you met Maria?" he said with a smile.

Maria was the name of my bride. It may sound confusing as I try to retell this story, but I knew exactly what he meant when he said that.

Maria Oliva wasn't only jaw-dropping gorgeous, she was beautiful in every single way. She was godly, smart, fun, mature. I had never met anyone like her before, and neither had my family. In a nice way, my dad was reminding me that the woman who was about to marry me was "out of my league." Maria was the best thing that ever happened to me, and he knew that.

"Thanks Dad. You're totally right."

And that was it.

The nerves left. I weighed the consequences of backing out and realized how dumb that would be. This decision couldn't be made on my feelings alone. If I was going to make a life-long covenant to this woman, in front of God, family, and friends, I was going to have to "man up" to a new level of responsibility. My life could no longer be just about me; but surprisingly, I was ready to make that decision.

Have you ever had a "man up" moment like that?

Have you ever had to make a decision that was bigger than yourself, yourfeelings, and maybe even your own future? I know the story of a young boy getting cold feet on his wedding day isn't the ultimate example; but it was a real moment of transition in my life. I remember making a consciousdecision to step up and step into the greater responsibility of God's calling.

What does it mean to be a man? Who is the ultimate example of manhood?

How about the God who became one?

Jesus is the God who became a man. We learn in Scripture that when in this world, Jesus is fully God and fully human. If we want to see what God looks like on a journey of manhood, we look no further than the God-man himself, Jesus Christ.

> *"And consider the example that Jesus, the Anointed One, has set before us. Let his mindset become your motivation. He existed in the form of God, yet he gave no thought to seizing equality with God as his supreme prize. Instead he emptied himself of his outward glory by reducing himself to the form of a lowly servant. He became human! He humbled himself and became vulnerable, choosing to be revealed as a man and was obedient. He was a perfect example, even in his*

death - a criminal's death by crucifixion! Because of that obedience, God exalted him and multiplied his greatness! He had now been given the greatest of all names! The authority of the name of Jesus causes every knee to bow in reverence! Everything and everyone will one day submit to this name - in the heavenly realm, in the earthly realm, and in the demonic realm. And every tongue will proclaim in every language: 'Jesus Christ is Lord Yahweh,' bringing glory and honor to God, his Father."

PHILIPPIANS 2:5-11 TPT

Over the next five chapters we are going to look at the life of Jesus as the perfect example and guide to manhood. We are going to examine five critical moments from His life that show us how to be a man. These moments will create a portrait of manhood in your own life that looks like Jesus. At the end of each section, there will be questions for reflections. If you are reading with other men, they will serve as discussion questions. My prayer is that you would finish this book with a vision of biblical manhood that will stir the faith that God has put inside you to live out your full potential. If you do this right and see yourself the way God sees you, your life won't be the only one that changes on an eternal level. You will leave a legacy of biblical proportions.

Let's take a look at how Jesus shows us that true manhood is saying "Yes" to the responsibility of God's calling on your life.

Discussion
& Reflection

1 What has been your greatest "man up" moment in life so far?

2 Why is it significant that we understand Jesus as the God who became man, not a man who became God?

ONE

BE WATCHFUL

Jesus the Shepherd

*"**Be watchful**, stand firm in the faith, act like men, be strong. Let all that you do be done in love."*

1 CORINTHIANS 16:13-14 ESV

I once stole a painting from church.

Well, actually, "lost" might be a better word.

Before you judge me, let me explain. I was a young associate pastor in charge of maintenance at my church, and it was my duty to paint the children's ministry room. As I was prepping the walls and taking down the pictures, I had to remove a particular painting that was getting on my nerves. Perhaps I just forgot to put it back up.

Maybe you have seen this picture? Does this sound familiar?

It is a portrait of the Son of God sitting on a rock. His golden surfer hair hangs just above his shoulders. His piercing blue eyes look straight into your soul, complimented only by a Mona Lisa smile. He has a beard that would make Chuck Norris jealous.

On His lap sits a small lamb that appears to be His personal pet. There is no name tag or collar around its neck, but you can tell for sure,

He knows its name.

This picture is beautiful and disturbing at the same time. It is beautiful because Jesus refers to Himself in the Scriptures as our "Good Shepherd." We feel safe in His strong, but gentle presence. We take comfort in the fact that He knows our name.

It is disturbing because it is not exactly biblically accurate. I'm not talking about His blue eyes; I mean the image of Jesus coddling a lamb. Jesus didn't have any real sheep in His ministry. He wasn't an actual shepherd; He was a carpenter and a rabbi. The people following Jesus were humans, not animals.

At first glance it may seem like a nice picture of Jesus. What's the harm?

> *"I tell you the truth, anyone who sneaks over the wall of a sheep-*
> *fold, rather than going through the gate, must surely be a thief and*
> *a robber! But the one who enters through the gate is the shepherd*
> *of the sheep. The gatekeeper opens the gate for him, and the sheep*
> *recognize his voice and come to him. He calls his own sheep by name*
> *and leads them out. After he has gathered his own flock, he walks*
> *ahead of them, and they follow him because they know his voice.*
> *They won't follow a stranger; they will run from him because they*
> *don't know his voice."*

JOHN 10:1-5 NLT

In the time of Jesus, everyone would have known what he was talking about when he described shepherds, sheep, gatekeepers, and sheep pens. Shepherding was a familiar occupation within the life of 1st century communities.

Imagine a terrain outside the city full of mostly desert, but scattered pastures. Shepherds would hike the dusty hillsides looking for areas their sheep could graze. They would carry a walking staff and often times a sling shot. Both were used for protection; but mostly for guiding the sheep. Sometimes they would scoot the sheep along with their staff. But, if the sheep wandered too far off, they could use their slingshots to accurately hit targets near the sheep to create a noisy ruckus and bring them back to the fold.

As the sun would go down, the shepherd's mind would turn from provision to protection. He would become more guarded as he kept watch over the sheep against the predators and threats that lurked in the shadows.

He would begin to direct his sheep toward a large communal sheep pen made of rocks. The rocks were stacked a few feet high and set up like a semi-circle with an opening at one end.

It was not unusual for multiple shepherds and flocks to use the same pen in the area for safety at night. There were plenty of predators such as wolves and mountain lions that would love to sink their teeth into a little lamb. After all the sheep were gathered, leaves and branches were laid across the top of the pen to create a covering. The shepherds might take turns keeping watch at night as they guarded their flocks from harm.

At dawn, the shepherds would walk out to the hillside and turn and face the sheep pen. With only their voice, they would call the sheep out of the pen to their side. One by one the shepherd would call the sheep by name. The sheep knew the voice of their shepherd. One by one they would leave the pen and head toward his voice. They recognized their shepherd's call. That was the voice that cared for them, guiding them toward green pastures and protecting them from the enemy.

When Jesus gives this incredible illustration, He is talking directly to the religious leaders of that day. He draws a parallel between the way He sees spiritual leadership and a good shepherd of his flock.

After Jesus explains this, the religious leaders still don't get it.

> "Those who heard Jesus use this illustration didn't understand what he meant, so he explained it to them: 'I tell you the truth, I am the gate for the sheep. All who came before me were thieves and robbers. But the true sheep did not listen to them. Yes, I am the gate. Those who come in through me will be saved. They will come and go freely and will find good pastures. The thief's purpose is to steal and kill and destroy. My purpose is to give them a rich and satisfying life. I am the

good shepherd. The good shepherd sacrifices his life for the sheep. A hired hand will run when he sees a wolf coming. He will abandon the sheep because they don't belong to him and he isn't their shepherd. And so the wolf attacks them and scatters the flock. The hired hand runs away because he's working only for the money and doesn't really care about the sheep. I am the good shepherd; I know my own sheep, and they know me, just as my Father knows me and I know the Father. So I sacrifice my life for the sheep. I have other sheep, too, that are not in this sheepfold. I must bring them also. They will listen to my voice, and there will be one flock with one shepherd. The Father loves me because I sacrifice my life so I may take it back again. No one can take my life from me. I sacrifice it voluntarily. For I have the authority to lay it down when I want to and also to take it up again. For this is what my Father has commanded.'"

JOHN 10:6-18 NLT

Jesus says a lot of truly remarkable things here. In fact, they are so inspiring that paintings of this passage fill up churches all over the world. If you aren't careful, you will miss the best part. Jesus declares, "I am the gate for the sheep."

The religious leaders and any of Jesus' original audience would have immediately pictured exactly what He is talking about.

Remember how I told you the sheep pens were semi-circle structures of stacked rocks? The entrance didn't have a gate that kept the predators out. There was no little door on hinges that he could close and lock tight. At night, the shepherd would occupy that space with his physical presence. He would literally become the gate to the sheep pen.

Jesus is saying that He stands as the gate to all His sheep.

If a lion, wolf, bear, or any predator wants to attack his sheep pen, they are going to have to go through that gate. They are going to have to take on the shepherd himself.

Jesus says that not only is He the Good Shepherd, but He is the very gate that protects the sheep. According to Jesus, there is only one way the enemy is going to get to His sheep.

Over His dead body.

Jesus wants you to know that He is watching over you. He says later in the chapter that "nothing can snatch you from His hand." You can trust Him. As you get to know His voice, He wants to help guide your life. Like He says in this passage, the enemy comes to steal, kill, and destroy, but He came to give you life. He will show you the way as you trust and follow Him.

Jesus is also showing you something about manhood. You are not His pet sheep that sits on His lap. He mentions a "gatekeeper" in the story. Yes, you are in His flock, but you are also becoming a shepherd like Him. Jesus is transforming you. Just as He is brave and watchful, He is changing you to be more like him. God wants you to be like Jesus and become a shepherd to those around you within your life. He wants to give you His strength to help you grow into manhood, and that requires stepping into more responsibility with what He has entrusted you.

You may start off as a shepherd boy or gate keeper with small responsibilities; but the more faithful you become, the more God will begin to trust you. He will not just trust you with opportunities, but with what He considers more valuable than anything - people. The more watchful you can become, the more God will send people into your life to serve and lead.

Are you single? Are you interested in ever finding a woman or having a family? Be watchful over the areas of your character so you can grow into a shepherd that He can trust with one of His daughters.

Do you enjoy business or entrepreneurship? Do you dream of running your own company or organization one day? Be watchful over your character. God wants you to grow in your responsibility so that He can trust you to lead, not just as a CEO, but as a shepherd to a flock.

Jesus shows us that true manhood is taking responsibility for what God has entrusted you, no matter the cost. Be on guard, keep your eyes on what He has already given you. Steward your life, relationships, and decisions like they all belong to God. He takes joy in training you up to become a Shepherd like Him.

You are not His pet. You are His shepherd in training.

Discussion & Reflection

1 In what areas of your life is God calling you to be more watchful?

2 What cost are you willing to pay as you take on more responsibility?

TWO

STAND FIRM

Jesus in temptation

*"Be watchful, **stand firm in the faith**, act like men, be strong. Let all that you do be done in love."*

1 CORINTHIANS 16:13-14 ESV

Just a few months before my 21st birthday, my life was beginning to un-ravel. A series of poor choices had led me so far from the way my parents raised me that it was hard to look in the mirror and see myself as a good man.

The truth was, I wasn't a good man. I was sinful and rebellious and now I was starting to feel the consequences. My life was full of pain and I was at a crossroads.

I got on my knees and prayed this prayer to God,

"Father, I have butchered the life you have given me. I have strayed so far from you and I am sorry. If you will take my life, you can have it. I'll give it back to you and serve you however you want."

It sounds dramatic, but that is exactly how that happened. I stood up from my knees a new man. I was forgiven and ready to take responsibility for the life God was entrusting to me. No turning back; I would live for Jesus now.

My journey didn't start off easy; it started with a test.

Not long after I prayed that prayer, God reminded me of a promise I had made to Him as a young boy. I had totally forgotten about it; but suddenly it was clear as day what I was supposed to do. I had promised God I would go to Bible College.

I knew I needed to keep my word and get to school. If God was testing me, I planned on obeying Him 100%. I went to the school website, and to my surprise, the new semester was starting in just a few weeks. That day I began the application process and started heading in a new direction.

I'm not going to lie to you; the first year following Jesus was very hard. I had just sold my car and it was going to cost me almost all of my money to cover tuition. I had to move out of my house where I lived with my closest friends and into a college dorm. I packed up and left to a city I had never been, to live on a college campus where I didn't know a single person.

I was broke, lonely, and susceptible to temptation.

"Jesus, full of the Holy Spirit, left the Jordan and was led by the Spirit into the wilderness, where for forty days He was tempted by the devil. He ate nothing during those days, and at the end of them He was hungry. The devil said to him, 'If you are the Son of God, tell this stone to become bread.' Jesus answered, 'It is written: "Man shall not live on bread alone."' The devil led him up to a high place and showed him in an instant all the kingdoms of the world. And he said to him, 'I will give you all their authority and splendor; it has been given to me, and I can give it to anyone I want to. If you worship me, it will all be yours.' Jesus answered, 'It is written: "Worship the Lord your God and serve Him only."' The devil led him to Jerusalem and had Him stand on the highest point of the temple. 'If you are the Son of God,' he said, 'throw yourself down from here. For it is written: "He will command his angels concerning you to guard you carefully; they will lift you up in their hands, so that you will not strike your foot against a stone."' Jesus answered, 'It is said: "Do not put the Lord your God to the test."' When the devil had finished all this tempting, he left him until an opportune time. Jesus returned to Galilee in the power of the Spirit, and news about Him spread through the whole countryside."

LUKE 4:1-14 NIV

After Jesus was baptized, the Holy Spirit led Jesus into the wilderness to be tempted. Yes, you read that correctly. It was God's idea for Him to go into the desert.

Did God know the devil would be out there seeking to tempt Jesus?

Yes.

Did God know that Jesus would be at His greatest point of human weakness?

Yes.

Was God setting His son up to fail?

No.

When you read the whole passage you see a powerful contrast between the first verse and the last. God is showing us something super important here. Jesus comes out of the season of wilderness testing stronger than when He went in. It clearly says that He was led by the Spirit into the wilderness, but He returned in the power of the Spirit.

"Jesus returned to Galilee in the power of the Spirit."

What happened between the time of being led by the Spirit into the wilderness and returning with new power?

Trials, tests, and temptations.

God knew exactly what would happen when He led Jesus into the wilderness. He knew it would be hard; He knew the Devil would be out there; and He knew Jesus would be tempted at His weakest moments. The

The Father wasn't setting up His son to fail.

He was setting Him up to win.

In case no one told you, following Jesus is the hardest thing you will ever do. I wish I could say it gets easier along the way, but I don't know if that will be true. I don't know God's will for your life. One thing I know for sure is that if the Father allowed His own Son to endure trials, tests, and temptations, they are coming your way too.

It sounds counter intuitive, but embrace these moments. Sometimes God allows them so you can take responsibility for your life and "man up." When you stand firm in your faith, you are becoming like Jesus.

Take courage that God knows what you can handle and what is too much. You are His son and He wants you to win. He wants you to be like Jesus and have victory over your sin and become stronger with every win.

> *"So, if you think you are standing firm, be careful that you don't fall! No temptation has overtaken you except what is common to mankind. And God is faithful; He will not let you be tempted beyond what you can bear. But when you are tempted, He will also provide a way out so that you can endure it."*

1 CORINTHIANS 10:12-13 NIV

The greatest temptation I have ever faced was a battle with lust. After I gave my life to Jesus, I still struggled with addictions and pornography. What did I expect? These things had been part of my life for most of my life. I think sometimes we forget that just because God frees us from our sin eternally, He doesn't always free us from the consequences right away.

I was nearly a year into my journey following Jesus, and I was just starting to consider volunteering at my church. It wasn't that I wasn't welcomed to serve, it was that I didn't feel strong. I knew I wasn't standing firm in my faith. Even though I knew in my heart I was forgiven, my ongoing struggle with pornography left me feeling weak.

At one point my pastor asked me to help with teaching the Bible to middle school boys. He graciously gave me the weekend to think about it. Was I really going to let my weakness rob me of the opportunity to be used by God to make a difference in someone's life? Manhood was calling. I needed to take responsibility for God's calling on my life at a new level.

I called my friend who lived on my college campus and I asked him to meet up with me to pray. When he showed up, he had no idea what I was about to drop on him; but I confessed it all.

I fell to my knees and asked him to pray for me that I would stand firm in my faith and overcome.

Not only did he pray for me, it turns out that he was struggling with the same thing! After we prayed together that day, we started to meet once a week with a group of guys with one laser-focused purpose: standing firm in our faith.

Something amazing happened in that group. We never missed a week for a total year, and all of us overcame our addictions to lust and pornography.

It was nothing short of a miracle. And, by the grace of God, I am still living that miracle today. At the time of writing this book I have gone 14 years clean of pornography.

I don't know what you're struggling with; but I know it's something. I know God has you in a process of becoming a man by transforming you to become like Jesus. That journey requires taking responsibility for your life and standing firm in your faith.

My advice to you is to get a group of guys around you so you can stand firm together. Even though I am walking in victory, the temptation is still there and lust is still a battle. Part of my routine is still meeting every week with a core group of guys to help each other stand firm in our faith. It can be hard to make that commitment and keep going even when you fail. That is why my group meets at 5:45 a.m. every Monday before we all go to work. That may sound crazy, but a lot of guys get up that early to go to the gym and work out. For me and my guys, standing firm in our faith is top priority.

God set Jesus up to win and He is going to do the same for you. Jesus faced the devil's test and won. He endured the trials and came out stronger. He faced temptation and stood firm.

Jesus shows us that when you take responsibility for your life and stand firm no matter the situation, you will always come out stronger. God never promised He would make life easy, but He did promise to always be with you.

Discussion & Reflection

"This is the message we heard from Jesus and now declare to you: God is light, and there is no darkness in him at all. So we are lying if we say we have fellowship with God but go on living in spiritual darkness; we are not practicing the truth. But if we are living in the light, as God is in the light, then we have fellowship with each other, and the blood of Jesus, his Son, cleanses us from all sin. If we claim we have no sin, we are only fooling ourselves and not living in the truth. But if we confess our sins to him, he is faithful and just to forgive us our sins and to cleanse us from all wickedness. If we claim we have not sinned, we are calling God a liar and showing that His word has no place in our hearts."

1 JOHN 1:5-10 NLT

1 **What are some of the trials, tests, and temptations going on in your life?**

2 **What does it look like to stand firm in your faith?**

3 **Have you taken responsibility to surround yourself with the people you need to stand firm?**

THREE

ACT LIKE A MAN

Jesus with a whip

*"Be watchful, stand firm in the faith, **act like men**, be strong. Let all that you do be done in love."*

1 CORINTHIANS 16:13-14 ESV

Remember that time Jesus flipped the tables, drove out the merchants and the animals, and went wild with a whip all over the temple courts?

Do you know where He got that whip?

He made it.

He didn't buy that whip. He didn't borrow that whip. He made it with His bare hands.

Let me ask you: how upset do you have to be to deliberately fashion together the materials required to make your own weapon?

No, no, no. You can't call that a weapon. Jesus didn't use weapons.

What else do you call it when you storm onto the temple mount during the most crowded day of the entire Jewish calendar and use an instrument like that to "drive out" all the corruption and send people running?

Call it what you want, but can we at least agree that Jesus was using a tool for a demonstration of force?

> "It was nearly time for the Jewish Passover celebration, so Jesus went to Jerusalem. In the Temple area he saw merchants selling cattle, sheep, and doves for sacrifices; he also saw dealers at tables exchanging foreign money. Jesus made a whip from some ropes and chased them all out of the Temple. He drove out the sheep and cattle, scattered the money changers' coins over the floor, and turned over their tables. Then, going over to the people who sold doves, He told them, 'Get these things out of here. Stop turning my Father's house into a marketplace!' Then his disciples remembered this prophecy from the

Scriptures: 'Passion for God's house will consume me.'"

JOHN 2:13-17 NLT

At the time of Jesus, Jerusalem and the temple would have been the most sacred place on earth. It was here that the temple stood tall for all the world to see and experience. This was the place that housed the very presence of God. The temple was the epicenter of holiness. It was so holy, in fact, that Jewish people from around the world made pilgrimages multiple times a year to worship and bring sacrifices.

Most travelers, especially those of far distance, didn't want the hassle of bringing their own animal for sacrifice on a long journey. Bringing an animal was challenging because there was a standard of quality required to be accepted as a sacrifice. The temple required the best. If your sacrificial animal, let's say a goat, scraped its leg on the journey to the temple it would immediately be considered "blemished" and unworthy. Rather than deal with the hassle and risk, it was more popular to buy an approved animal when entering the outer courts. However, this convenience came at a steep financial cost for the traveler, and a hefty profit for the merchant.

Also, within the outer courts were money changers. All Jewish males of age were required to pay an annual tax for the temple. In order to pay this temple tax, a particular currency was required. The exchange of common money for temple money was also done in the outer courts. However, this convenience also came at a cost to the traveler and gain for the bankers.

The Scripture says Jesus brought the whip during the week of the Passover Celebration. To say the temple area would have been crowded would be a drastic understatement. This was the most important celebration of the year.

Caravans of families full of grandmas, aunts, uncles, cousins, nephews, and nieces would all descend on Jerusalem in such a way that the population surged beyond ten times its normal size. It was rowdy, fun, holy, and dangerous all at the same time. Not only were Jewish families from all over the world in town for the festivities, so were many witnesses who were not of the same faith.

How were gentiles (non-Jews) welcomed to participate? There was a special outer court for them called the Court of the Gentiles. It was here in this outer area that they could draw close to the presence of God and witness the worship.

The Outer Court was the closest place non-Jewish visitors could get to the presence of God.

Are you putting all this together?

That fateful moment Jesus showed up to the temple courts, He couldn't believe His eyes. The corruption in the Outer Court/Court of the Gentiles was so bad it had crowded out the space specifically dedicated for the people who did not know or worship God. There was no room for the people who were furthest from God.

Jesus became "passionate." It was time for action.

I think sometimes we hear the phrase, "act like a man," and we immediately draw some comparison to acting like a girl. 1 Corinthians 16:13 isn't saying that at all. It's not saying stop acting like a girl; it is saying stop acting like a boy.

The journey of manhood is growing out of boyish ways and into the responsibility of a man. A boy doesn't see himself as responsible for others, only himself. Boyhood is the stage before you start putting other people's needs before your own. As a boy grows stronger and more mature, so does his ability to help other people - especially those that can't help themselves.

"When I was a child, I talked like a child, I thought like a child, I reasoned like a child. When I became a man, I put the ways of childhood behind me."

1 CORINTHIANS 13:11 NIV

I distinctly remember a time when I realized I was just a boy and needed a man's help. I was playing in my backyard when the neighborhood kids called me over to the fence and started picking on me. I must have been around nine years old at the time and there was a small wooden fence that separated my house from a family of four boys. Sometimes I would play with the younger boys who were my age, but the older boys weren't around much because they were much older.

"Hey, come here!" they called me to the fence.

I can't remember specifically what they wanted from me or why they were punking me, but I remember feeling very alone and very unsafe. I was scared because I was just a boy. The more they bullied me, the more I realized I could not stand up for myself. I needed someone who was bigger, a man, to take a stand for me.

"I'm going to get my brother!" I eventually yelled out with all my courage.

I ran into my house to get my older brother who was in high school. When I told him what was happening, he jumped to his feet and marched right out to that fence and the neighborhood boys scattered.

I have to admit, this story is a little embarrassing; but I think it makes my point. You can't be a boy and a man at the same time.

Boys step back. Men step up.

That day at the temple courts, when Jesus saw all that corruption, ripping people off, taking advantage of them, and crowding out the area that was supposed to be for the people far from God, He had enough. Somebody needed to take a stand for them.

So, He did what He had to do. He made a whip.

This wasn't a "temper tantrum" by a frustrated Jesus. This was a deliberate act of force from an authoritative leader within the religious system of that day. Jesus was taking a stand for all the people who couldn't take a stand for themselves.

Boys can't stand up for others with much success; that's the job of a man. That day by the fence, I remember not being able to stand up for myself and running away to find someone to fight for me.

Sometimes "manning up" means accepting the responsibility to help the people who can't help themselves. Jesus shows us that it is never just about standing up for ourselves. Biblical manhood accepts the call to stand with Jesus against the injustices of this world. When necessary, God will call you to do what men of strength can do that boys cannot.

Act like a man and fight for the people who can't fight for themselves.

Discussion & Reflection

1 What areas of your life are you still holding onto from your boyhood, even though it's time to act like a man?

2 Who has God placed in your life to serve until they are able to take care of themselves and others?

FOUR

BE STRONG

Jesus in a Storm

*"Be watchful, stand firm in the faith, act like men, **be strong**. Let all that you do be done in love."*

1 CORINTHIANS 16:13-14 ESV

When I was a youth pastor, I had the bright idea of taking a few students and a youth leader on a hiking trip to visit a waterfall. The hike was definitely more beautiful than it was strenuous, but it put us an hour away from civilization. When we finally arrived with our lunch and bathing suits, my youth worker confessed something that caught me a little by surprise,

"Yo, Justice, how deep is that water, because I don't know how to swim very well."

"You don't know how to swim?" I said. "How old are you, bro? Just stay in the shallow end and you'll be fine."

What I heard next from a 13-year-old student should have turned me right around and sent me back up the trail.

"Yo, I don't know how to swim either. Is the water cold? Maybe I'll just put my feet in."

I wish I had a picture to insert in this chapter; this place was beautiful. There were multiple waterfalls cascading off the cliffs into different swimming ponds. Beside the largest swimming area stood a cliff about one story high, just perfect for youth pastors to jump in and show off.

After lunch, I stood at the top of the boulder looking down for my first jump. I saw something I didn't expect. Remember the youth worker I told you about that said he couldn't swim that well? He was standing in the shallow end of the pond helping the student learn how to doggy paddle.

Almost like it was happening in slow motion, I watched the student slowly drift away from the youth leader and begin to sink. I couldn't believe what I was seeing. It was eerily quiet. He was thrashing around for help, but he couldn't be heard over the sound of the waterfall. I could tell from my vantage point on top of the boulder that there was nothing for him to grab onto to save himself.

What happened next only made things worse.

The youth worker left the shallow water in an attempt to reach the drowning student. It took less than two seconds for him to remember that he couldn't swim that well either. They grabbed each other for help, but quickly became each other's worst enemies, fighting each other to keep their heads above water. Both of them were going down quickly.

I stood at the top of the cliff, staring down in disbelief. No one was screaming; no sirens were ringing; but there were definitely two people drowning right beneath me.

I looked around for a rope or a large branch, but I was too far up. I had to jump in. I remember considering the consequences. I'm not a lifeguard. There was a good chance this wasn't going to end well for me either.

I jumped into the water next to them, took a deep breath, and swam underwater beside them. I knew I wasn't strong enough to hold them both above water; but maybe I could push them toward the shore.

Have you ever seen someone in a drowning panic? As I swam beside them they grabbed me and tried to pull me down to pull themselves up. Someone put their hand on top of my head and pushed me down. Instinctively, I swam even lower to break away.

I came up for air exhausted, but running out of time. I had to tread water because we were surrounded by rock face. There was nothing to grab onto. The shore was our only option.

I said a short prayer and took a deep breath. I knew this would be my last attempt. This time I swam underwater beneath them instead of beside them. I thought maybe I if I got under them I could push them without getting pulled down. Just as I got into position, my foot struck a rock.

A large rock lay just beneath my feet on the floor of the pond. It was just high enough for me to stand on and still reach my friends. Even though they were kicking and pushing me down, the rock didn't move, so neither did I. The giant rock was an unmoving foundation for me to stand on.

Everyone lived. The rock saved us.

I think it goes without saying, that was one of the scariest moments of my life. If it wasn't for that rock, I can only imagine what would have happened that day.

In a weird way it reminds me of a story of Jesus on the water.

> "Then he got into the boat and his disciples followed him. Suddenly a furious storm came up on the lake, so that the waves swept over the boat. But Jesus was sleeping. The disciples went and woke him, saying, 'Lord, save us! We're going to drown!' He replied, 'You of little faith, why are you so afraid?' Then he got up and rebuked the winds and the waves, and it was completely calm. The men were amazed and asked, 'What kind of man is this? Even the winds and the waves obey him!'"

MATTHEW 8:23-27 NIV

Jesus got into the boat first, then the disciples followed him. I think it's important we start there. The disciples weren't going somewhere they weren't supposed to go; they were following Jesus' lead. Sometime in their trip across the lake Jesus was tired enough to take a nap. It may seem weird to think of Jesus taking a nap, but remember that He was both fully God and fully human at the same time. Just like He got hungry, He also got tired.

The Scripture says a furious storm showed up suddenly. Out of nowhere the weather changed, the wind picked up and started tossing around the small sail boat. Water began coming over the sides and filling up the vessel to a dangerous level. At first the disciples thought they could handle it. They grew up on these waters. Maybe they had even been in storms like this before. Many of them were skilled fishermen and seamen. As the wind grew louder and stronger they started running out of options. They needed help and Jesus was somehow still asleep.

What did they expect Jesus to do when they woke Him up? Grab a sail and help them hold it against the wind? Pick up a bucket and start bailing water over the edge?

When Jesus wakes up, He does the unthinkable. He stands up and speaks to the storm itself.

He doesn't pray about it. He doesn't ask the disciples to gather together and make a prayer circle on the boat.

Jesus stands up and tells the storm itself, "Knock it off."

Instantly the wind and waves go calm and the boat begins to rest on the water. The disciples were left with only one thing to say, "What kind of man is this? Even the winds and the waves obey Him!"

What kind of man is that strong? Stronger than a storm? Stronger than creation?

The Creator Himself.

It is safe to say that the reason why the disciples asked what kind of man Jesus was, was because they didn't see Him as fully God. This hadn't been fully revealed to them yet.

Jesus wasn't acting strong. He wasn't acting like anything other than Himself. Jesus is strength. There is no limit to His power.

> "The Son is the image of the invisible God, the firstborn over all creation. For in him all things were created: things in heaven and on earth, visible and invisible, whether thrones or powers or rulers or authorities; all things have been created through him and for him. He is before all things, and in him all things hold together."

COLOSSIANS 1:15-17 NIV

Have you ever thought about taking responsibility for your strength? In the previous chapter we talked about acting like a man, but in this chapter we are not talking about acting like you are strong.

Jesus wasn't acting and He doesn't expect you to either.

You are strong.

You are strong because when you are born again your identity is joined with Christ. You are a new creation in which you are in Jesus and He is now in you.

In fact, there is nothing about you that is not strong. Even in your weakness, God says you are strong through Jesus. Oftentimes we think of the journey of manhood as becoming stronger, when in reality it is more about discovering the strength that you already have.

"Three different times I begged the Lord to take it away. Each time he said, 'My grace is all you need. My power works best in weakness.' So now I am glad to boast about my weaknesses, so that the power of Christ can work through me. That's why I take pleasure in my weaknesses, and in the insults, hardships, persecutions, and troubles that I suffer for Christ. For when I am weak, then I am strong."

2 CORINTHIANS 12:8-10 NLT

Maybe as you read this you don't feel strong. Maybe you feel weak and tired and you're just trying to keep your head above water. Maybe it is hard for you to get a real vision for your life and manhood, because you feel like a failure and your arms are tired from swimming.

Beneath you is a Rock.

Plant your feet on that Rock and stand straight up. The enemy would love to trick you and get you to believe the lie that your success depends on how well you can swim. It doesn't. Not even a little bit. Your success has everything to do with how strong that rock is beneath your feet.

When you are planted on the rock, it doesn't matter how well you swim, it only matters how well you can stand.

"For I can do everything through Christ, who gives me strength."

PHILIPPIANS 4:13 NLT

This is Scripture, not a motivational quote. It is a promise. You are stronger than you think because Jesus will never fail you. Biblical manhood means taking on the responsibility of strength that is available to you through God. Whatever it is you are facing today, humble yourself. You are not alone.

Discussion & Reflection

1 How is it possible to be weak and strong at the same time?

2 What areas of your life are going to require new humility to overcome?

FIVE

DO IT ALL IN LOVE

Jesus in the Garden

*"Be watchful, stand firm in the faith, act like men, be strong. **Let all that you do be done in love.**"*

1 CORINTHIANS 16:13-14 ESV

Where we live in Southern California is not that far from a theme park called Legoland. If you have ever been to Six Flags or Disneyland it is pretty similar, only it's totally designed for young kids.

Very young kids.

There are no giant roller coasters or adult attractions. There are a few small rides, but the whole place is mostly designed like a giant kid zone where young families can sit around and watch their kids play. The coolest part is this giant outdoor jungle gym - obstacle course - tree house. It is probably the size of half a football field. Surrounding this awesome monstrosity are benches and picnic tables where parents can sit back and let their kids run wild. There is only one way in and one way out; so unless someone gets stuck inside, it's pretty guarded and safe.

One day we are there with my 5 year old son, Logan, and his little brother, Carter. Logan is running around having a blast climbing the rock wall, running back and forth across the rope bridge, going down the slides and having the time of his life. He is quick to make friends and before long he is playing tag with some other kids, and my attention pretty much turns to my youngest son who is at the age where he is just starting to walk. After about half an hour, it's time to grab lunch as a family. I start to scan the giant playground to find my oldest son, but I'm having a hard time locating him. There are probably fifty or sixty kids running around on this giant playground, so I give Carter to my wife and start to head into the area.

"I'm going in!" I tell Maria. "There is only one way out of this area, will you keep an eye on the exit until I get back?"

I scale the cargo net to get to the first platform. Then I take the wobbly bridge over to the tunnel. A few more escalating platforms lead me to a high tower. On the other side I find a tall rope bridge and a cluster of different slides wrapping around in multiple directions.

I'm in there for what feels like 10 minutes and I still can't find my son. That's when I feel a low-grade panic start to build in my stomach. I think to myself, "Maybe I missed him? Maybe he went down one of these slides and he's with Maria near the exit?"

I pick a slide to leave the playground, but when I get to the exit, Maria doesn't have him.

Five more minutes go by, and still no Logan.

The low-grade panic is now growing into a full-blown terror. While Maria guards the exits, I'm going around asking parents if they have seen my son. With every passing minute my actions become more intense. I'm at the point now that I should recruit other parents to help me find him. I run toward the playground one last time, fly up the cargo net yelling his name,

"LOGAN!"

I'm on all fours now going up the tower until I can finally get to the rope bridge for a bird's eye view.

That's when I spot him. I found my son.

What I just described was possibly the most intense moment of my life. It is hard to put into words the magnitude of emotions happening in my mind and body at the same time. To call it an adrenaline rush wouldn't come close. It was probably closer to a heart attack.

The Scriptures give us a detailed account of Jesus' most intense moments. He had a lot of them; but I'm not sure anything can compare to the night before His death in the Garden of Gethsemane.

"Then Jesus went with his disciples to a place called Gethsemane, and he said to them, 'Sit here while I go over there and pray.' He took Peter and the two sons of Zebedee along with him, and he began to be sorrowful and troubled. Then he said to them, 'My soul is overwhelmed with sorrow to the point of death. Stay here and keep watch with me.' Going a little farther, he fell with his face to the ground and prayed, 'My Father, if it is possible, may this cup be taken from me. Yet not as I will, but as you will.' Then he returned to his disciples and found them sleeping. 'Couldn't you men keep watch with me for one hour?' he asked Peter. 'Watch and pray so that you will not fall into temptation. The spirit is willing, but the flesh is weak.' He went away a second time and prayed, 'My Father, if it is not possible for this cup to be taken away unless I drink it, may your will be done.' When he came back, he again found them sleeping, because their eyes were heavy. So he left them and went away once more and prayed the third time, saying the same thing. Then he returned to the disciples and said to them, 'Are you still sleeping and resting? Look, the hour has come, and the Son of Man is delivered into the hands of sinners. Rise! Let us go! Here comes my betrayer!'"

MATTHEW 26:36-46 NIV

I don't think it gets more intense than this. Jesus knows He only has a small window of time left before one of His best friends shows up to betray Him. He knows He is hours away from a torturous death on the cross.

He is so overwhelmed that He asks the disciples to pray for Him. Think about that for a second; God himself asked for prayer.

He falls to His face in private prayer. In Luke's Gospel it says His body was physically reacting to the stress in a way that His sweat looked like drops of blood.

*"My Father, **if it is possible**, may this cup be taken from me. Yet not as I will, but as you will."*

Jesus prays to His Father with a prayer anyone would ask. Is there any possible way to change the plan? Is this truly the only way?

He doesn't get the answer He hoped. Actually, the Gospel writers don't record any answer at all. He gets up to check on His prayer team only to find them asleep. He wakes them up because He needs their help, but then returns to prayer a second time.

At first read-through, you might not notice the difference between His first prayer and His second. The first time He went to His Father and He asked for Him to change His situation, to make another way.

Jesus' situation didn't change, so His prayer did.

*"My Father, **if it is not possible** for this cup to be taken away unless I drink it, may your will be done."*

In His second prayer, He is responding to the heartbreaking reality that His Father is leading Him somewhere He doesn't want to go. Because He didn't get an answer to the first prayer, He knows He must stick to the plan. At this point, not only has His prayer changed, so has His posture. Rather than asking the Father to change His plans, He resolves to embrace it.

Sometimes God doesn't change His plans; He just changes us.

What Jesus shows us here is that He has no equal anywhere else in history. No greater love has ever been shown. Jesus is the perfect example of manhood because He embodies a perfect love. It was God's love, nothing else, that gave Him the motivation and power to embrace the cross.

Jesus shows us how to do all things in love.

Without Christ, we have no hope for ourselves, and neither did God the Father. The primary way God reveals His love for us throughout the entire Bible is that of a Father who loves His children.

Without the cross, God the Father had no way of helping His lost kids come home to Him.

It may sound silly, but that day I lost my son at Legoland was probably the closest I will ever get to feeling God's heart for the lost. I can't begin to imagine how much worse and more intense it would have gotten the longer he stayed lost. I would have done anything to find him. That is how God see's a lost world, with a Father's heart.

It is important to know that Jesus was not surprised by the plan of salvation. The plan of salvation was just as much the decision of God the Son as it was God the Father. Jesus knowingly left His glory in Heaven to come to this world to rescue you. When He was left with no other options, He said to the Father,

"Over my dead body."

Over my dead body will Satan, sin, or death win this war for God's children. I will take on the full responsibility of every man, woman, child, and soul. I, the Creator, will enter the created world to do what only I can do and rescue them all back to the Father.

Jesus is the ultimate example of manhood because He was willing to pay the ultimate price for love.

And now Jesus invites you to join Him:

"If any of you wants to be my follower, you must give up your own way, take up your cross daily, and follow me."

LUKE 9:23 NLT

Discussion
& Reflection

1   **How is doing all things in love the epitome of manhood?**

2   **What areas of your life will continue to stay weak if you do not "man up" to do all things in love?**

DEAR FATHER, thank you for giving me life and free will. Today, I take responsibility for my past and everything I have ever done that has hurt someone you care about, including myself. I recognize that you have made a way for forgiveness and new life through Jesus and I humbly bow my knee to Him as Lord and Savior. Please fill me with the Holy Spirit so I can live a new life of power to follow your example. I want to be a man that you can trust and I am asking for your help on this journey of manhood to live worthy of your calling. Amen.

NOTES

NOTES

Made in the USA
Middletown, DE
19 November 2019

79020079R10042